DATE DUE			

T 50347

920
KNA

Knapp, Ron.

Top 10 basketball centers

LINDOP ELEMENTARY SD 92
2400 S 18TH AVE BROADVIEW IL

TOP 10 BASKETBALL CENTERS

Ron Knapp

SPORTS TOP 10

Enslow Publishers, Inc.

40 Industrial Road   PO Box 38
Box 398   Aldershot
Berkeley Heights, NJ 07922   Hants GU12 6BP
USA   UK

http://www.enslow.com

Library of Congress Cataloging-in-Publication Data

Knapp, Ron.
      Top 10 basketball centers / Ron Knapp.
          p. cm.—(Sports top 10)
      Includes bibliographical references (p.) and index.
      ISBN 0-89490-515-5
      1. Centers (Basketball)—United States—Biography—Juvenile
literature. [1. Basketball players.] I. Title. II. Title: Top
10 basketball centers. III. Series.
GV884.A1K63   1994
796.323'092'2—dc20
[B]   94-15808
                                              CIP
                                              AC

Printed in the United States of America

10 9 8 7 6 5

Photo Credits: Focus on Sports, pp. 6, 9, 11, 13, 14, 17, 23, 25, 38, 41, 43, 45; Mitchell Layton Photography, pp. 19, 21, 31, 33, 34, 37; Naismith Memorial Basketball Hall of Fame, pp. 26, 29.

Cover Photo: Mitchell Layton Photography.

Interior Design: Richard Stalzer.

CONTENTS

Introduction

What Does It Take To be a great basketball center?

The first quality is obvious. Ever since George Mikan, it's been important for a center to be tall. The athletes in this book are big men. When Hakeem Olajuwon was growing up in Africa, he hunched his shoulders because he didn't want people to notice his height. Later, like all the other centers, he realized that being tall is a huge advantage for a basketball player.

But there's much more to it than height. There are many seven-footers who have not achieved success in basketball. Great centers also have to be gifted athletes with a great deal of speed, agility, and skill.

They also have to be willing to work. None of these centers was a superstar the first time he stepped onto a court. They practiced endless hours to make it in college and in the pros.

It also helps to be tough. All these men have ignored pain and overcome injuries. A National Basketball Association season can include more than one hundred games. Over that amount of time an incredible amount of physical punishment can be handed out. Great centers have to keep coming back, giving their all, game after game.

Centers don't get pushed around. Playing center puts them right in the middle of the action. They can't sneak around or hang back. They're under the hoop shooting, blocking shots, and grabbing rebounds. They're in-your-face players. They want their opponents to be afraid of what they're going to do.

The ten centers in this book came from a variety of backgrounds. Two of them, Patrick Ewing and Hakeem

Olajuwon, weren't even born in the United States. Kareem Abdul-Jabbar had twenty brilliant seasons as a starting center in the NBA. Bill Walton had just one. Bill Russell played on nine championship teams. Bob Lanier never played on one.

Over the past fifty years, these ten giants have thrilled millions of sports fans. They've helped make basketball America's hottest, most exciting sport.

CAREER STATISTICS

Player	NBA Seasons	Games	FG%*	Rebounds*	Blocks*	Steals*	Points	Average
KAREEM ABDUL-JABBAR	20	1,560	.559	17,440	3,189	1,160	38,387	24.6
WILT CHAMBERLAIN	14	1,045	.540	23,924	—	—	31,419	30.1
DAVE COWENS	11	766	.460	10,444	488	599	13,516	17.6
PATRICK EWING	15	1,039	.509	10,759	2,758	1,061	23,665	22.8
BOB LANIER	14	959	.514	9,698	1,100	777	19,248	20.1
GEORGE MIKAN	9	520	—	—	—	—	11,764	22.6
HAKEEM OLAJUWON	16	1,119	.513	12,951	3,652	2,018	25,830	23.1
DAVID ROBINSON	11	765	.522	8,651	2,506	1,170	18,430	24.1
BILL RUSSELL	13	963	.440	21,620	—	—	14,522	15.1
BILL WALTON	10	468	.521	4,923	1,034	380	6,215	13.3

*Statistics for blocked shots and steals were not kept by the NBA until the 1973-1974 season. Statistics for rebounds were not kept until the 1950–1951 season. Mikan's field goal attempt totals are incomplete.

KAREEM ABDUL-JABBAR

A center's power is in his height, and his ability to jump. At seven feet two inches, Abdul-Jabbar dominated the courts.

KAREEM ABDUL-JABBAR

KAREEM ABDUL-JABBAR AND THE Los Angeles Lakers were the victims of the 1985 Memorial Day Massacre. They were hammered 148–114 by the Boston Celtics in the opening game of the NBA finals. Kareem looked tired and slow. By then he was thirty-eight years old. Fans wondered if he was just too old.

Abdul-Jabbar was humiliated by his performance. He apologized to his teammates and promised he would never let them down again. In the next game, he got 30 points and 17 rebounds, and Los Angeles won, 109–102. The Lakers took three of the next four as Kareem scored 26, 36, and 29 points. The old man had led his team to the title! "He's the most unique and durable athlete of our time, the best you'll ever see," said Pat Riley, the Lakers coach. "You'd better enjoy him while he's here."[1]

Kareem had always been a unique individual. Back in New York City, when he was still called Lew Alcindor, he was a quiet, intelligent boy who loved to read. By the time he was in seventh grade he was already six feet five inches tall, so he was invited to play basketball on the school team. Lew worked as hard at his basketball skills as he did at his studies. He lifted weights and practiced shooting until he had become a gifted player.

And Lew kept right on growing. By the time he had graduated from Power Memorial High School, he was just over seven feet tall. By then he had led his team to seventy-one straight victories. During his four years in high school, Power won ninety-five games and lost only six. In his final three years, his team lost only once.

Alcindor then moved to the University of California at Los Angeles (UCLA). His height, speed, and determination helped the Bruins dominate college basketball. They won three straight NCAA championships. In Lew's three years on the team, UCLA lost only twice.

Then Alcindor took his awesome talents to the NBA and the Milwaukee Bucks. He was Rookie of the Year for the 1969–1970 season. The next year he was the league scoring champ and MVP as he and Oscar Robertson took the Bucks to the NBA championship. By then his trademark shot, the "sky hook," was known and feared across the league. How can you stop a hook shot by a man who's seven feet two inches tall?

In 1971 after his conversion to the Islamic religion, Alcindor changed his name to Kareem Abdul-Jabbar, which means in Arabic "Noble and Generous Servant of the All-Powerful Allah (God)."[2] But the new name didn't make any difference in the way he played. Abdul-Jabbar was still one of the dominant players in the game. He won two more MVP awards with the Bucks before being traded to the Los Angeles Lakers in 1975.

Kareem was the superstar the Lakers needed. He helped turn them into the powerhouse that finally took the NBA championship in 1980, the year he won his sixth MVP Award. During the 1980s, Abdul-Jabbar and Magic Johnson made the Lakers one of the strongest teams in the history of the league. From 1980 to 1989, they appeared in eight NBA finals, winning five of them.

"Jabbar would never give up," said Maurice Lucas of the Portland Trail Blazers. "He's the most respected player in the league because he never bows his head. Such great inner strength. You may beat his team but you never beat him."[3]

KAREEM ABDUL-JABBAR

BORN: April 16, 1947, New York, New York.

HIGH SCHOOL: Power Memorial High School, New York, New York.

COLLEGE: UCLA (University of California, Los Angeles).

PRO: Milwaukee Bucks, 1969–1975; Los Angeles Lakers, 1975–1989.

RECORDS: Most seasons played, 20; Most points, 38,387; Most defensive rebounds in a season, 1,111; Most defensive rebounds in a game, 29.

HONORS: NBA MVP, 1971, 1972, 1974, 1976, 1977, 1980; NBA Rookie of the Year, 1970; Inducted into Naismith Memorial Basketball Hall of Fame, 1995.

For twenty seasons, Kareem Abdul-Jabbar set the pace for NBA play. In his first seventeen, he averaged more than twenty points per game.

WILT CHAMBERLAIN

THE PHILADELPHIA 76ERS HAD ALMOST blown the first game of the 1967 NBA finals. Now it was time for Wilt Chamberlain to take over. Sure, he was big and strong. But could he win a big game? He'd been playing in the NBA for seven seasons but his teams had never won a title.

This time Wilt and his Philadelphia teammates had lost a 19-point lead. The San Francisco Warriors had tied the game, and, with ten seconds to go, they had the ball. Rick Barry drove past Chet Walker. The only man between him and an easy basket was Chamberlain. Wilt slid over to stop the shot, but Barry slipped the ball to Nate Thurmond. Chamberlain lunged over Thurmond, who was already past him. Wilt got his hand on the ball, blocked the shot, and the buzzer sounded. Philadelphia won in overtime, 141–135.

Chamberlain, basketball's most famous scoring machine, only got 16 points in that game, but his team won. In Game Two, the 76ers buried the Warriors, 126–95; Wilt only scored 10 points. Fans wondered what was wrong. Why wasn't he taking shots? The answer was simple. Chamberlain wanted to win more than he wanted to score. "Sometimes," he said, "it's actually easier to play against a team that has one man doing most of the scoring."[1] In the finals, the strategy had worked. Philadelphia beat San Francisco four games to two, and Wilt was finally a champion.

Now that his teammates shared the scoring and Chamberlain played tough defense, his teams were much stronger. In the 1971–1972 season with the Los Angeles Lakers, he averaged only 14.8 points a game, but teammates like Jerry West and Gail Goodrich picked up the slack. With Wilt

WILT CHAMBERLAIN

Wilt Chamberlain puts all his energy into the pass. He was a tremendous presence on the basketball court.

concentrating on defense and rebounding, they also won thirty-three games in a row.

In the 1972 playoffs, the thirty-five-year-old Chamberlain had to go against Kareem Abdul-Jabbar, the twenty-five-year-old superstar of the Milwaukee Bucks. Wilt's defense was so tough that during one eleven-minute stretch he kept Kareem from scoring a single point. The Lakers whipped the Bucks, then beat the New York Knicks for Wilt's second NBA title.

But Chamberlain hadn't always been so unconcerned with his scoring. During the 1961–1962 season with the Philadelphia Warriors, he was on the floor for almost every minute of every game. He and the Warriors wanted to see how many points he could score. Their offense was designed to give him the ball every time they had possession. Wilt scored a record 4,029 points, an incredible average of 50.4 points per game. He had a 100-point game against the Knicks. But all his points didn't do the Warriors any good. They finished second to the Boston Celtics in the regular season, then were bumped out of the playoffs in the second round.

Even in high school, Chamberlain had been a scoring machine. He once had 90 points in a game for Philadelphia Overbrook. In his first game for the University of Kansas, he hit 52 against Northwestern.

Wilt was the first seven-footer to play pro basketball. Because of his height, he was called "Wilt the Stilt," a name he hated. Besides being tall, he was also extremely strong, so he overpowered his opponents. For seven straight years, he was the NBA's leading scorer. When he retired in 1973, he had 31,419 points.

Wali Jones, of the 76ers, isn't the only man who's sure of Chamberlain's place in the history of sports. "Everyone who knows the game of basketball," he said, "knows who really is the greatest."[2]

WILT CHAMBERLAIN

BORN: August 21, 1936, Philadelphia, Pennsylvania.

HIGH SCHOOL: Overbrook, Philadelphia, Pennsylvania.

COLLEGE: University of Kansas.

PRO: Philadelphia Warriors, 1959–1962; San Francisco Warriors, 1962–1965; Philadelphia 76ers, 1965–1968; Los Angeles Lakers, 1968–1973.

RECORDS: Most career rebounds, 23,924; Highest rebounds per game average, 22.9.

HONORS: NBA Rookie of the Year, 1960; NBA MVP, 1960, 1966, 1967, 1968; Elected to Naismith Memorial Basketball Hall of Fame, 1978.

The big men of the 1970s, Wilt Chamberlain and Kareem Abdul-Jabbar fight for the rebound.

DAVE COWENS

Dave Cowens helped power the Boston Celtics to NBA world championships in 1974 and 1976.

DAVE COWENS

IT WAS THE SIXTH GAME of the 1976 NBA finals, and the Boston Celtics were in trouble. With 7:25 left on the clock, the Phoenix Suns led, 67–66. A Suns victory would force a seventh and deciding game. The Celtics wanted to win the game—and the title—that day, so once again they turned to Dave Cowens.

The Boston center stole the ball, blazed downcourt, put in a layup, and drew the foul. He made the free throw, then scored two more baskets. That was it for the Suns. The Celtics won, 87–80.

Dave was only six feet eight inches tall, short for an NBA center. But he was much faster than the big men he played against. His coach, Tommy Heinsohn, bragged that Cowens could beat anybody in the league in a 100-yard dash. He chased players all over the court and had no trouble keeping up with speedy forwards who were used to slipping past most centers with no trouble. His long arms and leaping ability helped make up for his lack of height. He was an aggressive player who wasn't afraid to dive for the ball. When he made a good play, he and his teammates celebrated with headbutts. As he said, "I'm the one going a little bit nutty out there."[1]

As a high school student in Newport, Kentucky, Cowens was first known as a star on the swimming team. It wasn't until his junior year that he decided to try out for the basketball squad. By the time he was a senior at Florida State University, he was averaging 18.9 points per game.

The Celtics drafted Dave to replace Bill Russell, who had retired in 1969. Cowens was named co-Rookie of the Year for

1970–1971, and by the next season Boston was back on top. He only had 1,489 points, third-best on the team, but he knew scoring wasn't his job. He was supposed to be all over the court, harassing the opponents and getting the ball to his teammates. The strategy worked. It was almost impossible for other teams to keep up with Boston's fastbreaking style of play. In the 1974 finals, Dave held his own against Kareem Abdul-Jabbar and the Milwaukee Bucks. While keeping the Celtic offense moving, he scored 30 points in the third game. Then in the seventh game, he hit 28 points and 14 rebounds as Boston won, 102–87.

The next season the Celtics had a dazzling 68–14 record, and Cowens was named MVP. They were eliminated by the New York Knicks in the second round of the playoffs, but came back to win the title again in 1976. By then, the Celtics' quickness had made them the toughest defensive team in the league.

After the team had two poor seasons, Cowens was named player-coach in 1978. Boston struggled to a 29-53 record. The next season Dave decided to stick to just playing.

Rookie Larry Bird joined the team for the 1979–1980 season, and the Celtics were tough once again. They finished with the league's best regular season record, 63-19. After Boston lost to the Philadelphia 76ers in the playoffs, Cowens announced his retirement.

Jerry Lucas, of the New York Knicks, never forgot Cowens' speed. "One minute he's standing in front of you and the next he's gone, rolling in toward the basket or straight up in the air shooting his jumper. It's like he disappears."[2]

BORN: October 25, 1948, Newport, Kentucky.

HIGH SCHOOL: Newport Central Catholic, Newport, Kentucky.

COLLEGE: Florida State University.

PRO: Boston Celtics, 1970–1980; Milwaukee Bucks, 1982–1983.

HONORS: NBA co-Rookie of the Year, 1971 (Shared with Geoff Petrie, Portland Trail Blazers); NBA MVP, 1973; Elected to Naismith Memorial Basketball Hall of Fame, 1990.

Though the Boston Celtics were knocked out of the 1975 and 1977 playoffs, Cowens tied the playoff record both times with 20 defensive rebounds in a single game.

Patrick Ewing

WHEN PATRICK EWING WAS A little boy in Jamaica, he decided he wanted to be a professional soccer player when he grew up. If that didn't work out, he'd be an artist. "I loved to draw," he said. "I used to draw scenes and characters from Sunday comic strips."[1]

Lucky for the New York Knicks, Patrick's family moved to the United States when he was twelve years old. Too bad for the rest of the NBA.

Patrick learned to play basketball at his new home in Cambridge, Massachusetts. When he was in twelfth grade, he was already seven feet tall. He was also the starting center on the Cambridge Rindge & Latin High School team, the state champs three years in a row.

Ewing then played four years for the Georgetown Hoyas. In 1982, his freshman year, Georgetown made it to the NCAA championship game. In the opening minutes, Patrick was awesome, slapping away North Carolina's first four shots. But the referees called him for goaltending and the shots counted. With 2:37 to go, he sank a thirteen-footer. Georgetown was now only down by one, 61–60. After the Tar Heels missed, he rebounded and threw the ball downcourt. "Sleepy" Floyd hit a short jumper and the Hoyas led, 62–61, with a minute to go. But then Michael Jordan swished a sixteen-foot jumper to give North Carolina the national title, 63–62.

Two years later the Hoyas were back in the NCAA title game. This time Patrick had learned to block shots correctly, and Houston didn't have a chance. Georgetown won, 84–75, and Ewing was named the tournament MVP. That summer

With the greatest of ease, Patrick Ewing tosses in a shot against the New Jersey Nets.

PATRICK EWING

he played on the gold-medal-winning U.S. Olympic basketball team.

Patrick worked just as hard in the classroom as he did on the basketball court. He asked lots of questions and never skipped a class. He graduated with the rest of his class with a degree in fine arts.

After graduating from Georgetown, Patrick joined the New York Knicks in 1985. Despite missing thirty-two games with a knee injury, he scored 998 points and was named Rookie of the Year. When the Knicks won the Atlantic Division in 1988–1989, he averaged 22.7 points per game. His 2,347 points the next season were the most ever by a Knicks player.

Ewing was the starting center on the 1992 U.S. Olympic team. In the gold-medal game, he scored 15 points as Croatia fell to the "Dream Team," 117–85.

Over the next several seasons, Ewing continued to build on his exceptional career. In 1994 and 1999, he helped propel the Knicks to the NBA Finals, though the team fell short of winning a championship both times. In 2000, the Knicks traded Ewing to the Seattle Supersonics.

Today, Ewing is most often compared to the legendary Bill Russell. "They share an amazingly similar level of sensitivity," said John Thompson, his coach at Georgetown and Russell's teammate on the Celtics. "That's the biggest thing, their pride and their will to win. A lot of people have the will to play, but few have the will to win."[2]

PATRICK EWING

BORN: August 5, 1962, Kingston, Jamaica.

HIGH SCHOOL: Cambridge Rindge & Latin School, Cambridge, Massachusetts.

COLLEGE: Georgetown University.

PRO: New York Knickerbockers, 1985–2000; Seattle Supersonics, 2000– .

HONORS: NBA Rookie of the Year, 1986.

Early in his college career, Ewing developed a reputation for being quiet and aloof. Since then, however, fans have realized he's a fun guy who just enjoys privacy.

BOB LANIER

IF BOB LANIER HAD LISTENED to his elementary coach, he never would have played basketball. Even though he was already five feet eleven inches tall when he was eleven years old, Bob could not make the team. His coach said he was too clumsy.

But another coach at a Boys Club near his home in Buffalo, New York, encouraged him to keep trying. So Bob learned to skip rope to improve his coordination. He also practiced long hours in the gym. After a while, his skills began to improve in several sports. He pitched a no-hitter in baseball and won the club Ping-Pong championship. By the time he got to high school, he was a star basketball player, too.

Then he turned tiny St. Bonaventure University into a basketball giant in the late 1960s. His size—6 feet 11 inches and 260 pounds—helped him to dominate on the court.

In 1970, he earned All-American honors by leading the Bonnies to twenty-six consecutive victories. They beat Davidson, North Carolina State, and Villanova in the NCAA tournament. It looked like the Bonnies had a real shot at the title until Lanier ripped the ligaments in his right knee. He wound up in the hospital and St. Bonaventure lost to Jacksonville, 91–83.

The knee healed, and Lanier was drafted by the Detroit Pistons of the NBA. During ten seasons in Detroit, he established himself as the greatest center in Pistons history. When he finally left the team, he had more points (15,488), field goals (6,276), and rebounds (8,063) than any other Detroit

BOB LANIER

Bob Lanier uses his height to get one over the Washington Bullets.

player. His career scoring average of 22.7 points per game is still the best ever for a Piston.

Unfortunately for Bob, the Pistons in the 1970s were one of the weakest teams in the NBA. During the 1971–1972 season he scored 2,056 points and totaled 1,132 rebounds, a Detroit record. But the team's record was a dismal 26-56. While he was with the Pistons, they made the playoffs only four times, then never made it past the second round.

Playing on such mediocre teams, Lanier never got the attention from the fans that centers like Bill Walton and Kareem Abdul-Jabbar received. But at the 1974 All-Star Game, he demonstrated that he was one of the finest athletes in the game. Playing against other great players, he had 24 points and 10 rebounds to win MVP honors.

Halfway through the 1979–1980 season, when the Pistons had won only sixteen games, Lanier was traded to the Milwaukee Bucks. Finally he was with a winner. After he joined the Bucks, they went 20-6 and won the Midwest Division title.

Three years later Milwaukee dropped the Boston Celtics in four straight playoff games before losing to the Philadelphia 76ers. By then Bob was thirty-four years old and in his thirteenth year as a starting center in the NBA.

When the veteran star retired in 1984, he had 19,248 points. Abdul-Jabbar was glad he would no longer have to face Lanier. "There's no way you can shut him off," he said. "He's a great center."[1]

Bob Lanier

BORN: September 10, 1948, Buffalo, New York.

HIGH SCHOOL: Bennett High School, Buffalo, New York.

COLLEGE: St. Bonaventure University.

PRO: Detroit Pistons, 1970–1980; Milwaukee Bucks, 1980–1984.

HONORS: #1 NBA Draft Pick, 1970; Elected to Naismith Memorial Basketball Hall of Fame, 1992.

Trying to get past all-time great Elvin Hayes, Lanier drives toward the hoop.

GEORGE MIKAN

George Mikan was the nation's top scorer two years in a row at DePaul University.

SIX-FOOT TEN-INCH GEORGE MIKAN WAS the big man who changed basketball forever. At first his teammates ridiculed him for his size and his thick glasses. In 1945, Rhode Island State coach Frank Keaney said his team's quickness and skill would leave Mikan "stumbling over his own feet."[1] The big man took the insult as a challenge, and he had one of his greatest games, scoring 53 points as DePaul University won, 97–53.

It was Ray Meyer, the DePaul coach, who turned Mikan into a basketball player. As Meyer explained, "A big man could score more points by accident than a little one could trying hard."[2] George might have been big, but nobody tried harder than he did. In college, to improve his coordination, he lifted weights, boxed, danced, and ran every day. Then he shot 250 right-handed hooks and another 250 left-handed.

All the work paid off. Mikan became basketball's first superstar. He was a three-time All-American at DePaul and the nation's leading scorer in his junior and senior years. In the 1945 National Invitational Tournament, he averaged 40 points a game as DePaul took the title.

George signed a $62,000 contract to play for the Chicago American Gears in the National Basketball League. As a rookie, he led them to the 1947 NBL championship. After the Gears left the league in 1948, Mikan wound up on a new team—the Minneapolis Lakers. With "Big George" at center, they switched leagues from the NBL to the Basketball Association of America. A year later they were part of the new National Basketball Association. In eight seasons, the Lakers had six championships. During three of those seasons, Mikan was the league's leading scorer.

The only way to stop Mikan was to stall. During a game in 1950, the Fort Wayne Pistons passed and passed and passed to waste time and keep the ball away from him. The strategy worked: George got just 15 points, and the Pistons won the lowest-scoring NBA game ever, 19–18.

Basketball today is a much different game because of Mikan and the big men who followed him. Players rely much more today on jump shots because it's easier to shoot over tall opponents. The free-throw lane has been widened from six to twelve, and now to sixteen feet so big men can't crowd near the basket. The goaltending rule was put into effect so that tall players couldn't slap away shots coming down toward the hoop. The NBA has a 24-second clock to prevent teams from stalling.

Nobody was surprised in 1950 when the Associated Press named Mikan the greatest basketball player of the first half of the twentieth century.

Mikan's height gave him a big advantage over his opponents, but he was a tough competitor who wasn't afraid of getting bumped. During his career, he suffered two broken legs as well as fractured bones in both feet, and a broken nose, wrist, thumb, and three fingers. He also required 166 stitches for various injuries.

"George Mikan was the greatest competitor I've seen," said Laker teammate Bud Grant, later coach of the Minnesota Vikings National Football League team. "He played hurt. He played when he'd had no sleep because of our travel schedule. And he always played at one speed—top."[3]

GEORGE MIKAN

BORN: June 18, 1924, Joliet, Illinois.

HIGH SCHOOL: Joliet Catholic, Joliet Illinois; Quigley Prep, Chicago, Illinois.

COLLEGE: DePaul University.

PRO: Chicago American Gears, 1946–47; Minneapolis Lakers, 1947–1954, 1955–1956.

HONORS: Elected to Naismith Memorial Basketball Hall of Fame, 1959.

Before there were the Los Angeles Lakers of Magic Johnson, there were the Minneapolis Lakers of George Mikan. He helped lead them to NBA championships in 1950, 1952, 1953 and 1954.

HAKEEM OLAJUWON

IT LOOKED LIKE THE 1986 Boston Celtics were about to cruise to another NBA title. They edged the Houston Rockets, 112–110, in the opening game, then buried them, 117–95. Hakeem Olajuwon, the Rockets center, was embarrassed and angry. But he laughed when reporters asked him if the Celtics would sweep the series. He said there was no way that could happen.

Hakeem was right. In the third game, his crucial free throw helped Houston beat Boston, 106–104. Then after another Celtic win, his 32 points and 14 rebounds paced a 111–96 Rocket victory. In the sixth game, he stole the ball three times in a row from Boston's Bill Walton. He followed up two of the steals with slam dunks. But that wasn't enough to stop Larry Bird and the Celtics. Boston won the game—and the title—114–97.

It was a disappointing end to the series, but very few fans had expected Olajuwon and the Rockets to come that far. Just as almost nobody had ever expected a tall, skinny kid from Africa to become a superstar center in the NBA.

Hakeem had left Nigeria in 1980 to enroll at the University of Houston. By then, the seven-foot-tall seventeen-year-old had given up soccer and handball for basketball. He practiced hard, exercised, and lifted weights until he was strong enough and good enough to earn the center spot on "Phi Slama Jama" as the Cougar team was known.

In the 1983 NCAA finals, Olajuwon scored 20 points against North Carolina State University. He also blocked so many close shots that the Wolf Pack was forced to take jump shots from the outside. But the long shots started to fall in,

HAKEEM OLAJUWON

Seven-foot Hakeem Olajuwon uses his size and strength for rebounding as well as scoring. In 1993 and 1994, he was named NBA Defensive Player of the Year.

and North Carolina State won on a desperation shot at the buzzer.

After three years of college ball, Olajuwon joined seven-foot four-inch Ralph Sampson who was with the NBA's Rockets. The fans called the two giants the "Twin Towers." In Hakeem's rookie year, he had 974 rebounds and 220 blocked shots.

Three years later he scored in double figures in all but one regular season game. In every year with the Rockets, he has averaged more than 20 points a game.

Olajuwon's long arms have helped him become one of the league's toughest shot-blockers. His height and jumping ability allow him to play tough against the other big men, while his speed lets him keep up with most of the smaller players. "I take pride in playing defense," he said. "I like to score, but defense is my first love."[1]

By 1993, Olajuwon was the highest-paid center in NBA history. He was also the third player to record more than 10,000 points, 5,000 rebounds, and 1,000 steals, assists, and blocked shots. The others were Julius Erving and Kareem Abdul-Jabbar.

Finally, in 1994 Hakeem became a champion when the Rockets beat the New York Knicks four games to three in the NBA finals. That same year he was also the first player to be named regular season MVP, playoff MVP, and Defensive Player of the Year.

Ever since his college days, Hakeem has been making life miserable for his opponents. Many of them probably wish he had kept playing soccer and handball in Africa. Nobody wants to put up a shot against him. It's a lot like shooting over a big tree. As Jim Killingsworth, former Texas Christian coach, explained, "It's hard to think about making a shot when it may get shoved down your throat."[2]

BORN: January 21, 1963, Lagos, Nigeria.

HIGH SCHOOL: Moslem Teachers College, Lagos, Nigeria.

COLLEGE: University of Houston.

PRO: Houston Rockets, 1984– .

RECORDS: Most blocks in an NBA career, 3,459.

HONORS: #1 NBA Draft Pick, 1984. NBA MVP, 1994; NBA Finals
MVP, 1994; Defensive Player of the Year, 1994.

Through determination and hard work, Hakeem Olajuwon has become one of basketball's greatest centers.

DAVID ROBINSON

With the first pick in the 1987 NBA Draft, the San Antonio Spurs gambled on David Robinson. Their two-year wait for the Naval Academy graduate paid off.

NOBODY IN THE NBA LIKES to shoot against David Robinson. The San Antonio star goes up, up, and up to slap the ball away. Of course, it helps to be seven feet one inch tall. His strength and speed have also helped "Mr. Robinson" become one of the most feared shot-blockers in the league.

When he was young, David was a great student. He even built his own television and computer. He had a wide variety of interests, such as literature, music, carpentry, tennis, and baseball. He played basketball for a year when he was in junior high school, but didn't even go out for the high school team until he was a senior. His friends at Osbourn Park High School convinced him to try out for the team. Since he was six feet seven inches tall, they were confident he'd be a great player.

His friends were right, of course. Later, when he was a freshman at the United States Naval Academy, David earned a spot on the team as a reserve center. He never started a game that year, but by the end of his sophomore season he was one of the best-known centers in the nation.

His shooting, shot-blocking, and rebounding led Navy to the 1986 NCAA tournament for the first time in twenty-five years. His team made it to the quarterfinals before losing 71–50 to Duke. That was the year he set a college record of 207 blocked shots. That was more than the total for any team except Louisville, the national champions.

The next season he was named College Player of the Year. During his four years at the Academy, the team's record was 106–25, its best ever.

Robinson was drafted by the San Antonio Spurs in 1987,

but they had to wait two years before he could play. Because he had gotten a free education at the Naval Academy, David had to serve as a lieutenant for two years at a naval base in Georgia. During that time he was on the gold-medal-winning U.S. Olympic basketball team in 1988.

When he finally joined the San Antonio Spurs in 1989, he was the highest-paid rookie in NBA history. With him on the team at last, the Spurs' record improved from 21-61 to 56-26. His 983 rebounds and 1,993 points earned him Rookie of the Year honors.

In the next season, he led the NBA in rebounds with 1,063. In 1991–1992, despite missing fourteen games with a broken thumb, he had 305 blocked shots, tops in the league. He also finished fourth in rebounding (929) and fifth in steals (2.3 per game).

After the thumb healed, Robinson became the youngest NBA star on the 1992 U.S. Olympic basketball team. It was the first time professionals had been allowed to take part in the Olympic basketball competition. David and teammates like Magic Johnson, Larry Bird, Karl Malone, and Michael Jordan destroyed all opposition on their way to the gold medal.

Robinson continued to excel at his game throughout the 1990s, but was never able to carry the Spurs deep into the playoffs. In 1997 though, help arrived in the form of fellow center Tim Duncan. Together with Duncan, Robinson and the Spurs dominated the NBA playoffs by 1999. They won a championship that year by eliminating Patrick Ewing and the New York Knicks in five games.

Cotton Fitzsimmons, former coach of the Phoenix Suns, said Robinson "is the greatest impact player the league has seen since Kareem Abdul-Jabbar." He compared Johnson, Bird, and Jordan to Robinson. "They're all MVPs," he said, "but this guy is more."[1]

DAVID ROBINSON

BORN: August 6, 1965, Key West, Florida.

HIGH SCHOOL: Osbourn Park, Manassas, Virginia.

COLLEGE: United States Naval Academy.

PRO: San Antonio Spurs, 1987– .

HONORS: #1 NBA Draft Pick, 1987; NBA Rookie of the Year, 1990; NBA
MVP, 1995; Defensive Player of the Year, 1992.

Robinson displays his power of concentration.

BILL RUSSELL

Bill Russell was a member of the legendary Boston Celtics dynasty. Between 1957 and 1969, they won eleven NBA World Championships. They lost in 1958 and 1967.

BILL RUSSELL

BILL RUSSELL WAS THE GREATEST player on the greatest pro team of them all, the Boston Celtics of the 1960s. Nobody was a more intimidating presence on the court. He once told an opponent to bring salt and pepper to a game because he was going to make him eat basketballs.

In the 1968 playoffs, Russell led the Celtics back from a three-games-to-one deficit to force a final deciding game against Wilt Chamberlain and the Philadelphia 76ers. Throughout the second half, Russell allowed Chamberlain to take only two shots. With time running out, Boston led by 2 points, but Philadelphia had the ball. Chet Walker drove for the tying basket, but Russell slapped the shot away. The 76ers got the rebound and missed a shot. This time Bill grabbed the ball, clinching the Celtics victory.

Boston went on to beat the Lakers that year for the NBA championship. It was one of eleven titles in just thirteen years. The first had come in 1957 when Bill totaled 32 rebounds in the deciding game against the St. Louis Hawks. The last one came in 1969. By then, Russell was thirty-five years old. Problems with his legs had sent him to the hospital. "His knees really bothered him," said teammate Bailey Howell. "So he didn't even practice. He just played the games. But once he got his knees warm, he was all right until the game was over. Then they were stiff and sore again."[1]

Bill had been a skinny, clumsy child growing up in Oakland, California. At first he was a poor basketball player in high school, but he kept trying—and he kept growing. By the time he was a senior at McClymond High School, he was six feet five inches tall and a fine ball handler.

By the time he was a junior at the University of San Francisco, he had grown another four inches. He learned to use his awesome jumping ability to block shots and grab rebounds. His team won fifty-five games in a row and two National Collegiate Athletic Association championships (1955 and 1956).

After leading the United States to an Olympic gold medal in 1956, he joined the Celtics. For the next thirteen years, any time he was on the floor he dominated the boards. For ten seasons he averaged more than 20 rebounds a game. His long arms and quickness made him the best shot-blocker in the game. Elvin Hayes called him "the Ghost." "You wouldn't see him anywhere, and he'd come out of nowhere to block your shot."[2]

Russell blocked the lane and made sure nobody got an easy basket against the Celtics. He was never concerned with scoring points himself. If he could frustrate the offensive efforts of the other teams and then rebound the ball and get it to his teammates, he knew there was no way Boston could lose.

Even though Bill loved to play basketball, he was usually very nervous and excited before a game. His stomach would be so upset that he almost always vomited before he left the locker room.

By the time he won his last two titles with the Celtics, Russell was not only the team's center—he was also the coach. That made him the first African-American coach to win a championship in a major league sport.

During his professional career, Russell's greatest rival was Chamberlain. Wilt had fine statistics and usually out-scored Russell, but when their teams met, the result was almost always the same. "I've been in seven playoffs with Boston when it all came down to the final game," Chamberlain said, "and Boston won six."[3]

BILL RUSSELL

BORN: February 12, 1934, Monroe, Louisiana.

HIGH SCHOOL: McClymond, Oakland, California.

COLLEGE: University of San Francisco.

PRO: Boston Celtics, 1956–1969.

HONORS: NBA MVP, 1958, 1961, 1962, 1963, 1965; Elected to
Naismith Memorial Basketball Hall of Fame, 1974.

Russell reaches toward the sky for a rebound. He holds the single-game record for most rebounds in one half. He pulled down 32 against the Philadelphia Warriors in 1957.

BILL WALTON

THE PORTLAND TRAIL BLAZERS WERE eighteen seconds away from their first NBA championship. They led the Philadelphia 76ers, 109–107, in the sixth game of the 1977 finals. In the closing seconds of play, the 76ers missed three shots. Then Bill Walton, the Blazers center, knocked the ball away, and the buzzer sounded. As the Portland crowd went berserk, Walton ripped off his sweat-drenched jersey and threw it into the stands.

That was Walton's greatest moment as a professional athlete. If he had stayed healthy, he might have been the greatest center in the history of the NBA.

Bill loved to compete. When he was growing up in La Mesa, California, he and his brothers were always jumping, trying to be the first to be able to touch the living room ceiling. Bill finally made it. By the time he was the star center for Helix High School, he could touch the ceiling with his elbow.

Helix won forty-nine games in a row. Walton then led UCLA to the longest winning streak in the college's history. Over three years, the Bruins won eighty-eight straight games. In 1972 and 1973 they were the NCAA champions. For three years, Walton was an All-American and the college Player of the Year.

Then, in 1977, he took the Trail Blazers to the NBA title. Before beating the 76ers, Bill's awesome shot-blocking helped Portland sweep Kareem Abdul-Jabbar and the Los Angeles Lakers in the Western Conference finals.

However, by the 1977–1978 season, injuries had begun to take their toll. A bone spur on his ankle, a broken toe, a fractured wrist, and tendinitis limited his playing time. Even

BILL WALTON

The Portland Trail Blazers used their first round draft pick wisely in 1974. Bill Walton led the team to their first NBA Championship in 1977.

though he missed two months of the season, he won the MVP award. Over the next four seasons, he only played fourteen games.

Finally, in 1985–1986, he was back for a complete season with the Boston Celtics as back-up center. He did well enough to earn the NBA Sixth Man Award, as the best bench player in the league. He was an important part of the Celtics' championship season. But by then his ankle hurt so badly he could barely walk, let alone play basketball. He retired after playing only ten games in 1986–1987.

Walton was an awesome, unforgettable sight on the court, even though for just a short time. He was a huge man (six feet eleven inches) with a head of thick, bright red hair. Sometimes it was so long he wore it in a ponytail. His freckled face often sported a scraggly beard. Off-court he wore sandals and jeans and often rode his bike to games. Once he was arrested for protesting against American involvement in the Vietnam War.

Some fans thought Walton was a pretty weird guy. But when he grabbed the ball, his opponents knew they were in trouble. He was a complete team player and one of the best passers in the game. If none of his teammates was open, he would throw up a jumper or dribble toward the basket himself.

"Bill was a rebel,"[1] admitted John Wooden, his coach at UCLA. But he said Bill's fierce determination to win improved the play of his teammates. "There have been many great players in the game, but not many great team players. Walton is a very great team player."[2] Wooden said nobody could start a fast break as fast as Walton.

Jack Ramsay, the Portland coach, respected his center as an athlete—and as a man. "Bill Walton is the best player, best competitor, best person I have ever coached.[3]

BILL WALTON

BORN: November 5, 1952, La Mesa, California.

HIGH SCHOOL: Helix High School, La Mesa, California.

COLLEGE: UCLA (University of California, Los Angeles).

PRO: Portland Trail Blazers, 1974–1979; San Diego Clippers, 1979–1984; Los Angeles Clippers, 1984–1985; Boston Celtics, 1985–1987.

HONORS: NBA MVP, 1978; Elected to Naismith Memorial Basketball Hall of Fame, 1993.

Walton's career was ended prematurely due to injury.

NOTES BY CHAPTER

Kareem Abdul-Jabbar

   1. Billy Packer and Roland Lazenby, *The Golden Game* (Dallas: Taylor Publishing Company, 1991), p. 198.

   2. Editors, Salem Press, *Great Athletes* (Pasadena, Calif.: Salem Press, 1992), vol. 1, p. 7.

   3. Packer and Lazenby, p. 165.

Wilt Chamberlain

   1. Roland Lazenby, *The NBA Finals* (Dallas: Taylor Publishing Company, 1990), pp. 109–110.

   2. Ibid., p. 111.

Dave Cowens

   1. Roland Lazenby, *The NBA Finals* (Dallas: Taylor Publishing Company, 1990), p. 142.

   2. Ibid., p. 143.

Patrick Ewing

   1. Neil Cohen, "A Dream Come True," *Sports Illustrated for Kids* (November 1992), p. 56.

   2. Alexander Wolff, *100 Years of Hoops* (Birmingham, Ala.: Oxmoor House, 1991), p. 90.

Bob Lanier

   1. Art Berke (editor-in-chief), *The Lincoln Library of Sports Champions,* vol. 10 (Columbus, Ohio: Frontier Press Company, 1985), p. 66.

George Mikan

   1. Bill Gutman, *The Pictorial History of Basketball* (New York: Gallery Books, 1988), p. 44.

   2. Alexander Wolff, *100 Years of Hoops* (Birmingham, Ala.: Oxmoor House, 1991), p. 132.

   3. Ibid.

Hakeem Olajuwon

   1. Associated Press Dispatch (May 9, 1994).

2. Ron Knapp, *Sports Great Hakeem Olajuwon* (Hillside, N.J.: Enslow Publishers, 1992), p. 34.

David Robinson

1. Jack Clary, *The NBA: Today's Stars, Tomorrow's Legends* (Rocky Hill, Conn.: Great Pond Publishing, 1992), p. 86.

Bill Russell

1. Roland Lazenby, *The NBA Finals* (Dallas: Taylor Publishing Company, 1990), p. 115.

2. Alexander Wolff, *100 Years of Hoops* (Birmingham, Ala.: Oxmoor House, 1991), p. 138.

3. Art Berke (editor-in-chief), *The Lincoln Library of Sports Champions*, vol. 16 (Columbus, Ohio: Frontier Press Company, 1985), p. 13.

Bill Walton

1. Billy Packer and Roland Lazenby, *The Golden Game* (Dallas: Taylor Publishing, 1991), p. 149.

2. Alexander Wolff, *100 Years of Hoops* (Birmingham, Ala.: Oxmoor House, 1991), p. 110.

3. Roland Lazenby, *The NBA Finals* (Dallas: Taylor Publishing Company, 1990), p. 165.

INDEX